SPACE TECH

HIGH-TECH SPACE SCIENCE

MEGAN KOPP

CRABTREE
Publishing Company
www.crabtreebooks.com

Author: Megan Kopp

Editors: Sarah Eason, John Andrews, and Petrice Custance

Proofreader and indexer: Wendy Scavuzzo

Editorial director: Kathy Middleton

Design: Paul Myerscough, Paul Oakley, and Jane McKenna

Cover design: Paul Myerscough

Photo research: Rachel Blount

**Production coordinator and
  Prepress technician:** Margaret Amy Salter

Print coordinator: Margaret Amy Salter

Consultant: David Hawksett

Produced for Crabtree Publishing Company by Calcium Creative.

Library and Archives Canada Cataloguing in Publication

Kopp, Megan, author
      Space tech / Megan Kopp.

(Techno planet)
Includes index.
Issued in print and electronic formats.
ISBN 978-0-7787-3602-8 (hardcover).--
ISBN 978-0-7787-3616-5 (softcover).--
ISBN 978-1-4271-1990-2 (HTML)

      1. Astronautics--Technological innovations--Juvenile literature.
2. Astronautics--Juvenile literature. I. Title.

TL793.K645 2017   j629.4   C2017-903593-2
                                                 C2017-903594-0

Library of Congress Cataloging-in-Publication Data

CIP available at the Library of Congress

Crabtree Publishing Company
www.crabtreebooks.com   1-800-387-7650

Printed in Canada/092017/PB20170719

**Published in Canada
Crabtree Publishing**
616 Welland Ave.
St. Catharines, Ontario
L2M 5V6

**Published in the United States
Crabtree Publishing**
PMB 59051
350 Fifth Avenue, 59th Floor
New York, New York 10118

**Published in the United Kingdom
Crabtree Publishing**
Maritime House
Basin Road North, Hove
BN41 1WR

**Published in Australia
Crabtree Publishing**
3 Charles Street
Coburg North
VIC, 3058

CONTENTS

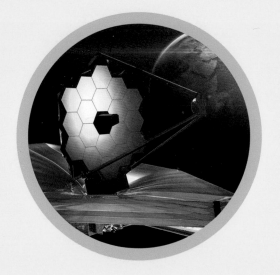

FAR OUT!

Human beings have always been fascinated by the universe. We are curious by nature. We want to explore the unknown. We want to discover new worlds. Space travel allows us to push the boundaries of our knowledge. It tests the limits of our abilities. Space travel allows us to question our role in the universe. It helps us understand the history of our solar system. Space travel allows brilliant minds to create solutions to problems.

UP, UP, AND AWAY

It is challenging to build a ship to go into space. Spaceships must be able to exit Earth's **gravity**, survive extreme temperatures, and handle the impact of space debris. In many cases, they must also be able to make the return trip to Earth.

When it is a manned mission, many other challenges arise. Humans are needy beings. Every day, we must meet our basic needs for food, water, shelter, and oxygen. Spaceships have to fulfill these needs. They must also protect astronauts from the hazards of space. The risks of space travel are magnified when astronauts step outside their protected environment. This is sometimes necessary for maintenance and repair of the spacecraft.

Stepping out into space requires the right knowledge and the right tech.

Scientists and researchers must plan for every possibility. In the case of the Apollo 13 mission to the Moon, brainstorming was done on the fly. An oxygen tank exploded before the **lunar** landing. The crew's living area was losing oxygen. One of the astronauts famously reported, "Houston, we've had a problem." Scientists and engineers on the ground then had to come up with a quick solution to save the lives of the crew.

Discovery, exploration, problems, and solutions all go hand-in-hand with space technology. It is a new frontier that brings out the inventive spirit in people. It is an exciting challenge waiting to be met.

Days are long and full of wonder when astronauts leave Earth's gravity behind as they head for the Moon and beyond.

GETTING THERE AND BACK

The Chinese invented the first rockets in the 1200s. They were called fire-arrows. These rockets were not very reliable. Many exploded when launched. Others flew off without a sense of direction and landed in the wrong place. Today, rockets stay on course. They go fast enough to escape Earth's gravitational pull.

ROCKET SCIENCE

A rocket is a vehicle that contains everything needed to put a **payload** into space. A payload can be anything from satellites to astronauts to spacecraft that will travel to other planets or moons. Rocket engines are devices that produce the **thrust** necessary to lift a rocket into space. The rocket must also be stable in flight. Large rockets heading into space need **systems** that stabilize the rocket and allow it to change course while in flight.

Large rockets that can carry a spacecraft into space are heavy. To gain enough speed, they need a lot of fuel, or **propellant**. The storage containers for propellant become so large, they weigh down the rocket even more. A solution was invented to strap small rockets on top of bigger ones. When the small rocket uses all of its propellant, the empty rocket shell drops off.

Orion *is NASA's new spacecraft. It will carry astronauts farther into the solar system than has ever been possible before.*

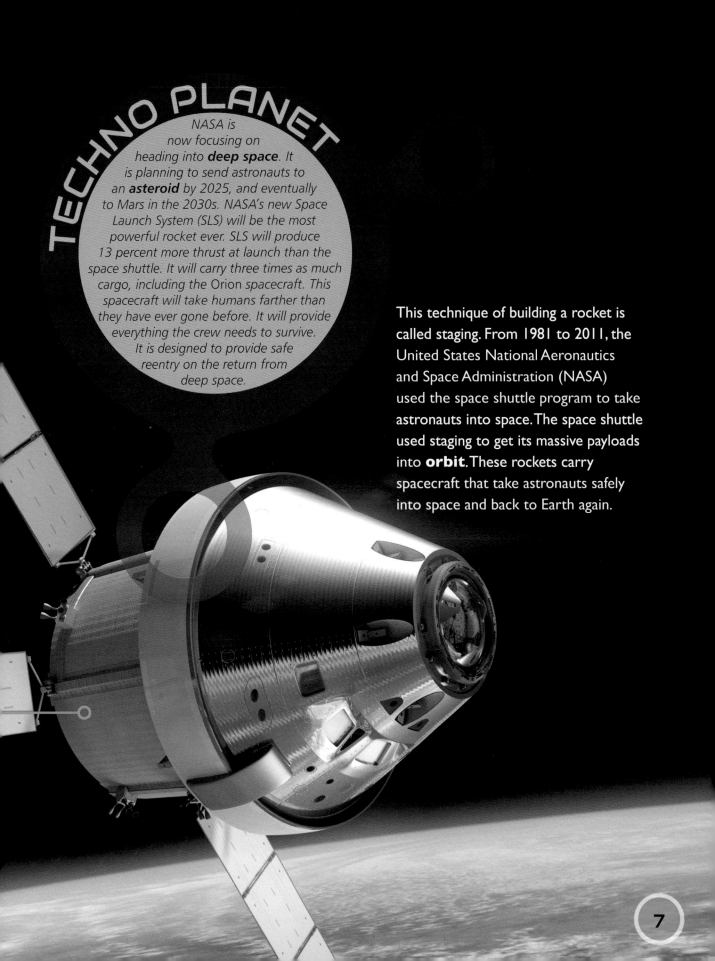

TECHNO PLANET

NASA is now focusing on heading into **deep space**. It is planning to send astronauts to an **asteroid** by 2025, and eventually to Mars in the 2030s. NASA's new Space Launch System (SLS) will be the most powerful rocket ever. SLS will produce 13 percent more thrust at launch than the space shuttle. It will carry three times as much cargo, including the Orion spacecraft. This spacecraft will take humans farther than they have ever gone before. It will provide everything the crew needs to survive. It is designed to provide safe reentry on the return from deep space.

This technique of building a rocket is called staging. From 1981 to 2011, the United States National Aeronautics and Space Administration (NASA) used the space shuttle program to take astronauts into space. The space shuttle used staging to get its massive payloads into **orbit**. These rockets carry spacecraft that take astronauts safely into space and back to Earth again.

SPACE STATIONS

A space station is a large spacecraft that orbits around Earth. It is a home where astronauts live. Space stations are also science labs. There have been 13 different space stations since 1971. Salyut 1, built by the **Soviet Union,** was the first to launch. It was a test station for living and working in space. It orbited the Earth 2,929 times during its 175 days in space. Salyut 1 was intentionally crashed into the Pacific Ocean after its work was done.

LABS IN THE SKY

The first United States space station was called Skylab. It was launched in 1973. Skylab continued to test life in space. Many new technologies were developed. Special showers, toilets, sleeping bags, exercise equipment, and kitchen facilities were designed to work in very weak gravity conditions. Skylab was meant to stay in space for several years after its work was done. The plan changed in 1979 when Skylab reentered Earth's atmosphere and broke apart.

The Soviet Union launched another space station, named Mir, in 1986. During its 15 years in orbit, Mir hosted 125 **cosmonauts** and astronauts. The astronauts came from 12 different countries. Mir saw 23,000 scientific and medical experiments and the first crop of wheat grown in space. Cosmonaut Valeri Polyakov spent nearly 438 days aboard Mir, from 1994 to 1995.

While he carries out his work, astronaut Stephen K. Robinson is connected to the Canadarm2 attachment of the International Space Station (ISS).

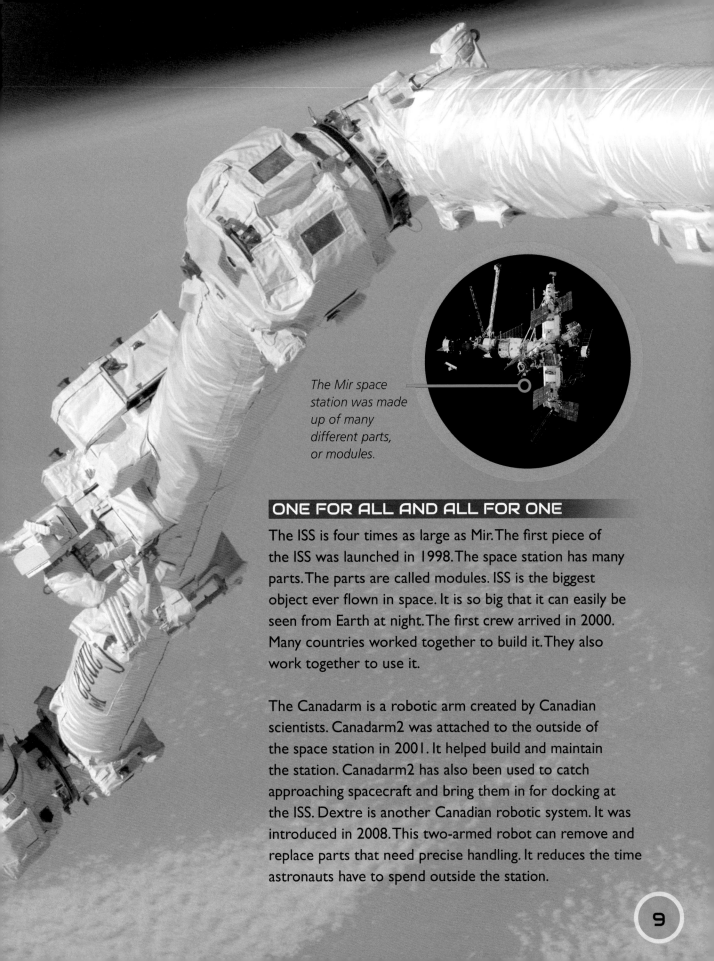

The Mir space station was made up of many different parts, or modules.

ONE FOR ALL AND ALL FOR ONE

The ISS is four times as large as Mir. The first piece of the ISS was launched in 1998. The space station has many parts. The parts are called modules. ISS is the biggest object ever flown in space. It is so big that it can easily be seen from Earth at night. The first crew arrived in 2000. Many countries worked together to build it. They also work together to use it.

The Canadarm is a robotic arm created by Canadian scientists. Canadarm2 was attached to the outside of the space station in 2001. It helped build and maintain the station. Canadarm2 has also been used to catch approaching spacecraft and bring them in for docking at the ISS. Dextre is another Canadian robotic system. It was introduced in 2008. This two-armed robot can remove and replace parts that need precise handling. It reduces the time astronauts have to spend outside the station.

SPACE SUITS

Space is a tough place to survive. There is no oxygen to breathe. The temperature in space can be extremely hot or extremely cold. There are often deadly levels of radiation. An astronaut in everyday clothing would die within minutes. That is why they need space suits. The first pressurized suits were worn by high-altitude test pilots. Ever since then, scientists have been designing better, more effective suits for astronauts traveling into space.

INSIDE AND OUT

Today's astronauts wear normal clothing while working on the ISS. The space station is a controlled environment with air to breathe and regulated temperatures. Outside of the station, astronauts use two very different space suits. One is for takeoff and landing. The other is for extravehicular activity, or spacewalks.

The Sokol space suit is used on the Soyuz spacecraft that takes astronauts from Earth to the ISS and back. It is a rescue suit, designed to keep astronauts alive in case of an accidental loss of pressure in the spacecraft. Outside the spacecraft, astronauts wear an Extravehicular Mobility Unit (EMU). This suit protects them from extreme temperatures, radiation, low **atmospheric pressure**, **micrometeoroids**, and other hazards.

An EMU has 13 layers and includes everything an astronaut needs to survive during a long spacewalk. It has everything from a drink bag and oxygen supply to communications equipment and a urine-collecting garment.

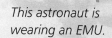

This astronaut is wearing an EMU.

Some of the technology used in space suits can be used for other applications, as well. For example, astronauts wear an inner suit with a pattern of thin plastic tubes. Cold water is pumped through the tubes to keep the astronaut cool. This technology is now used to make cooling systems for firefighters, steel workers, and other workers who have to wear heavy protective clothing in hot situations.

LIVING IN SPACE

The ISS has a series of systems to control the environment and provide life support within the station. Water is a precious thing, especially in space. All wastewater on the ISS is recycled, including urine. Wastewater is also purified to make drinking water and to generate oxygen.

FEED ME!

Space food has changed over the years. The first astronauts ate pureed food squeezed out of tubes. Freeze-dried food came in bite-sized cubes. It was not very appealing. Space food needs to be compact, lightweight, nutritious, and tasty. It needs to be sticky because crumbs and food particles float away in a weightless environment. It also has to keep for long periods of time. There are no refrigerators in space. New packaging materials block the moisture and oxygen that make food go bad. This technology usually finds its way into packaged foods in your supermarket.

WORK AND PLAY

Astronauts on the ISS have many tasks. Some members of the crew spend a lot of time on science experiments. They study how different fluids, metals, and other materials react in space without the effect of gravity. On Earth, delicate crystals are pulled out of shape by gravity. In space, these crystals can grow bigger and keep a much more regular shape. Many new medicines are created using crystals called proteins. Using space to study these crystals and understand how they are shaped helps scientists create new medicines for diseases such as diabetes or cancer.

Playing with your food is allowed in space. Some might even call it scientific research!

In 1992, astronaut Mae Jemison became the first African-American woman in space.

Exercise is an important part of an astronaut's day. Due to weightlessness, bone and muscle loss are common hazards of space travel. Astronauts exercise for about two hours a day. They use equipment designed for a weightless environment. This includes treadmills, a **resistive** exercise device, and a cycling machine. The astronauts have to strap themselves to each machine so they do not float away! The exercises on the ISS help people on Earth. Older people who have the bone-wasting disease **osteoporosis** can strengthen their bones with similar exercises.

While on the space station, members of the crew have time to relax and play. Looking at Earth is a popular pastime. Sunsets and sunrises happen every 45 minutes above Earth's atmosphere. Canadian astronaut Chris Hadfield used some of his spare time to record a David Bowie song. Hadfield's version of *Space Oddity* has more than 35 million views on YouTube!

MOON COLONY?

The man in the Moon may soon have company! The Moon's untapped natural resources are huge incentives for settlement. There are enough minerals and energy sources to support a colony and to ship minerals back to Earth. The Moon is also the perfect stepping stone for further exploration in our solar system and beyond.

FIRST THINGS FIRST

Before a colony can be built on the Moon, we need to get people back up there. Between 1969 and 1972, 12 astronauts walked on the Moon. No one has landed on the Moon since 1972. It takes an enormous amount of energy to get outside of Earth's gravity. This makes the trip very expensive. Rockets need to be constructed to carry astronauts, equipment, and materials to the Moon.

The astronauts would have to build more permanent structures on the Moon after they land. At first, they would need to rely on resources that have been brought from Earth for their survival. The goal is to become self-sufficient. Humans need water, food, shelter, and oxygen to survive.

This is NASA's idea of what an outpost on the Moon may look like in the near future.

NASA has proof that there is water on the Moon. However, it is not the same liquid we find in our rivers and lakes. Water and oxygen are locked in lunar soil. There is also water ice inside Moon **craters**. Technology is being developed to get these resources out of the ground.

The gravity on Earth pulls everything down. Strong materials are needed to build tall structures that do not collapse. The gravity on the Moon is just one-sixth of that on Earth. This means buildings could be made six times taller than on Earth using the same materials. However, a Moon shelter comes with its own difficulties. There is no air on the Moon, so a shelter would need to be pressurized with air, like a pumped-up balloon, so people could breathe. The shelter's walls would have to be strong enough to withstand that pressure. Also, the shelter would need to protect astronauts from extreme temperatures and radiation. At first, lightweight shelters will be shipped from Earth. After that, a colony might have to use Moon rock and soil to make their own building materials.

TECHNO PLANET

Energy production is a big reason why a colony on the Moon is drawing attention. There is a lot of sunlight at the lunar **poles**, which is perfect for harnessing solar energy. This energy could be used on the Moon or sent back to Earth. The lunar soil also contains a relatively high amount of Helium-3 gas. Very little of this gas is found on Earth. Helium-3 is believed to be an environmentally friendly fuel for energy generation.

SPACE PROBES

A space probe is an unmanned spacecraft that collects scientific information. This information is sent back to Earth to be studied. Many probes study Earth or measure properties of space. Others use telescopes or other instruments to study distant planets, stars, and galaxies. Probes can include flyby missions, orbiters, landers, and rovers.

THE LEAP INTO SPACE

Sputnik 1 was the first probe to go into space. It was launched in 1957 by the Soviet Union. Explorer 1 was the first United States probe. It was launched in 1958 to study Earth from space. Mariner 2 was the first probe to study another planet, Venus. It confirmed that the planet is very hot. In 1971, Mariner 9 became the first probe to orbit another planet when it arrived at Mars after 167 days flying in space.

EARLY MARS EXPLORATION

Mars, "the red planet," has fascinated humans for centuries. In 1965, NASA's Mariner 4 flew past it. The space probe sent back images of a landscape filled with craters. Two more missions flew by in 1969. They showed a dry landscape with no vegetation.

Flyby missions were then replaced by orbiters and orbiter-landers. More data streamed back to Earth. NASA's Viking missions landed on Mars in 1976. They took pictures of the entire planet and gathered surface samples to test for signs of life. The gases in the Martian atmosphere were also studied. Although no life was discovered, there were signs that water was present in the past. In 1997, the Mars Global Surveyor arrived for nearly 10 years of research. Mars Pathfinder carried the first simple rover.

The Voyager mission opened up new views of space as it observed the planet Jupiter close up.

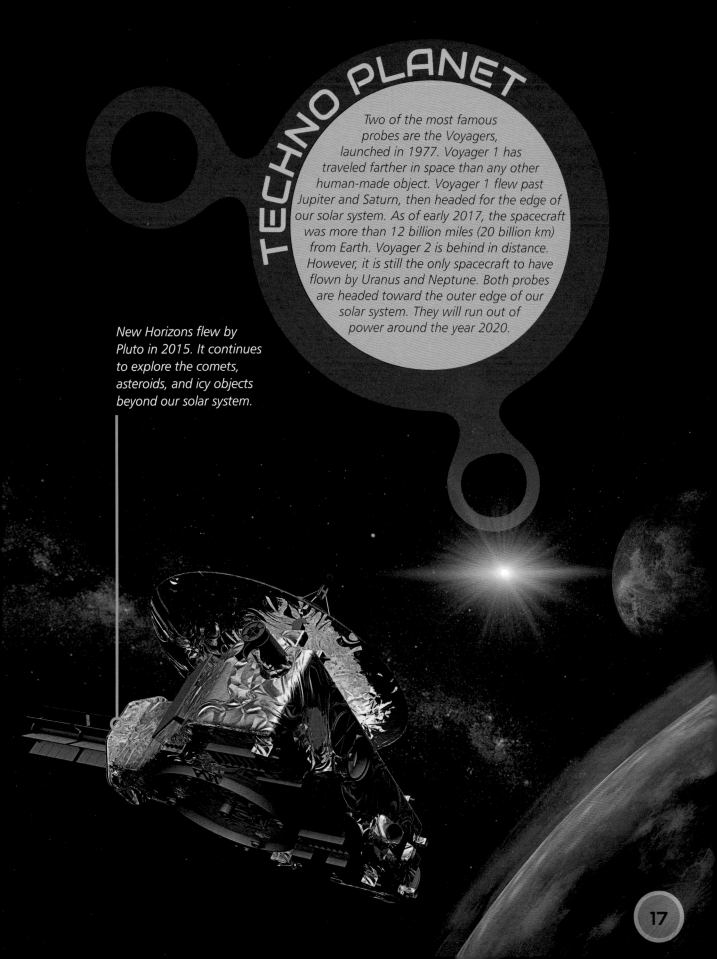

TECHNO PLANET

Two of the most famous probes are the Voyagers, launched in 1977. Voyager 1 has traveled farther in space than any other human-made object. Voyager 1 flew past Jupiter and Saturn, then headed for the edge of our solar system. As of early 2017, the spacecraft was more than 12 billion miles (20 billion km) from Earth. Voyager 2 is behind in distance. However, it is still the only spacecraft to have flown by Uranus and Neptune. Both probes are headed toward the outer edge of our solar system. They will run out of power around the year 2020.

New Horizons flew by Pluto in 2015. It continues to explore the comets, asteroids, and icy objects beyond our solar system.

PREPPING FOR LIFE ON MARS

The Moon will be a training ground and maybe a launching point for human life on Mars. NASA has a long-term plan to send humans to Mars. Why Mars? Earth and Mars have a lot in common. Both planets have seasons, mountains, valleys, dunes, rocks, riverbeds, and polar ice caps that contain frozen water. There are places on Mars where temperatures are similar to winter temperatures in Antarctica. Mars has a day length just half an hour longer than ours. The big difference? Mars is a new frontier.

EXPLORING THE RED PLANET

First came Spirit and Opportunity, then the mobile science laboratory rover named Curiosity. Powered by a bank of solar cells on its upper surface, each Mars Exploration Rover (MER) is able to communicate with orbiting probes and directly with Earth. Each rover comes with cameras and special tools for exposing rock and looking at it closely, like a **geologist** with a hammer and a magnifying glass. Curiosity landed on Mars in 2012. It carried a tool for chemical analysis of the materials collected. The Alpha Particle X-Ray Spectrometer measures the chemical **elements** in the rocks and soils on Mars. It is funded by the Canadian Space Agency.

The Mars 2020 rover mission will look for evidence of past life on the red planet. It will collect soil and rock samples. The rover will store these samples in a particular spot, from where they can be collected and returned to Earth by a future mission.

"Eat your vegetables!" Learning to grow healthy food will be important for space pioneers on Mars.

All the data collected will be put to use. It is thought that astronauts could be heading to Mars by 2030. They will have travel meals similar to those found on the ISS. The food will need to last a long time because the journey could take up to eight months. NASA is teaming up with a private company to explore the possibility of making food using **three-dimensional (3-D)** printers. If this is successful, food could be printed out as needed. This would allow for longer trips into deep space. NASA also realizes that, one day, tools or even spacecraft parts could be 3-D printed, too. As an experiment, a tool called a wrench has been 3-D printed on the ISS.

Mars rovers such as this will clear the way for humans to set foot on the red planet.

SATELLITE SPACE

A satellite is an object that moves around a larger object. Earth is a satellite because it moves around the Sun. It is a natural satellite. When people talk about satellites, they are usually talking about artificial satellites.

WHAT IS AN ARTIFICIAL SATELLITE?

Artificial satellites are launched into space by a rocket. They circle around Earth or something else in space. Satellites must be placed at least 100 miles (160 km) above Earth's surface so that they are not slowed down by Earth's atmosphere. There are thousands of human-made satellites.

All satellites have an **antenna** and a power source. The antenna sends and receives information. Some satellites have cameras. The first satellite picture of Earth came from NASA's Explorer 6 in 1959. Other satellites have scientific **sensors**. They can gather information about Earth's weather or climate. They may also collect data from the solar system and the universe.

TALKING AND FINDING OUR WAY

Some satellites are used for television signals, phone calls, and the Internet. They can be used to improve access to health services for people living in remote and isolated locations, such as northern Canada. Other satellites are used for security and defense. Canada's first space mission was the Alouette 1. It studied an upper layer of Earth's atmosphere to improve long-range communication for Canada's armed forces.

Satellites have become important for **navigation**. Most new automobiles have GPS to help drivers find their way. GPS stands for Global Positioning System, which is a navigation system that sends signals from at least 24 satellites. These satellites orbit more than 12,500 miles (20,200 km) above Earth. GPS began as a military navigation tool. It is still operated by the U.S. Air Force.

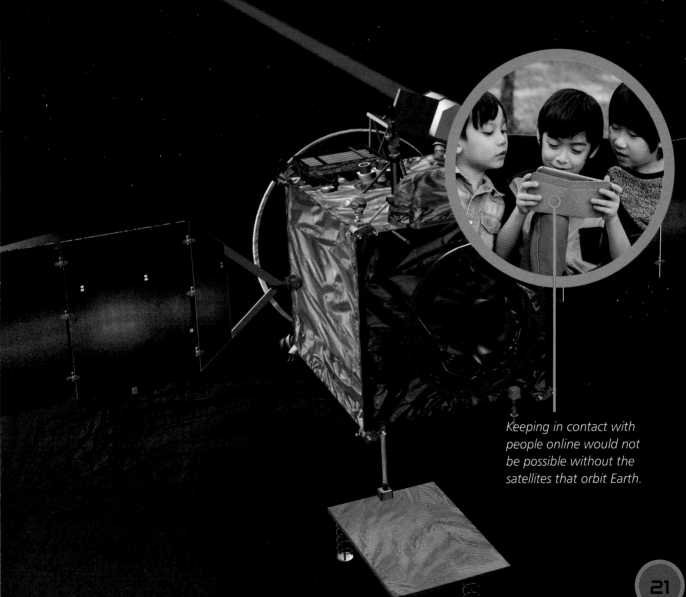

Satellites provide everything from Internet connections on Earth to the communication systems necessary for NASA's journey to Mars.

STUDYING EARTH

Satellites are valuable tools for studying Earth, its atmosphere, and its climate. Satellites allow scientists to get a global view of glaciers and snow, soil moisture, ocean currents, and the concentration of **greenhouse gases** in the atmosphere. They also help scientists monitor changes in our ecosystems. Satellites have better than a bird's-eye view. They can be used to observe changes in the condition and health of forests and national parks. They can identify changes over time in coastlines, wetlands, and wildlife habitats. Satellites can also measure pollution and monitor natural disasters.

Keeping in contact with people online would not be possible without the satellites that orbit Earth.

LOOKING DEEP

Edwin P. Hubble was an American astronomer. He studied the planets, stars, and space. He made important discoveries about the universe. The Hubble Space Telescope was named after him.

FAR OUT FACTS

The Hubble Space Telescope is an enormous telescope. It is as long as a tanker truck. On Earth, it weighs as much as two large elephants. In space, it weighs almost nothing.

Hubble is a big eye in the sky that was launched into space more than 25 years ago. It travels at an altitude of about 353 miles (568 km) above Earth. It goes around Earth 15 times a day.

TECHNO PLANET

Bigger, newer, brighter—that is the James Webb Space Telescope. It was named after a former NASA director. It will launch in October 2018 on an Ariane 5 rocket. It will not orbit Earth. Webb will orbit the Sun, in a spot on the far side of the Moon. This space telescope will see a light that is different from the light that Hubble sees. It will help NASA learn more about deep space. The Webb will be a joint operation between NASA, the European Space Agency, and the Canadian Space Agency.

The Webb telescope is seven times more powerful than Hubble. Scientists will view things in space that have never been seen by humans before.

The Hubble Space Telescope uses mirrors to collect information about light in space. It takes pictures and makes measurements of objects as close as the Moon and as far away as the most remote galaxies. Hubble has seen stars being born. It has seen them die. It has seen comets crashing on distant planets.

Hubble makes space discoveries. It found moons orbiting Pluto. It helped scientists estimate the age of the universe—almost 14 billion years old. Hubble turned 25 years old in 2015. It has been fixed several times in space. It will not be fixed again. For now, Hubble continues to take beautiful pictures of deep space.

Hubble has opened our eyes to the endless possibilities of space. It has done its job well.

These towering pillars of gas and dust are where stars are born. The Hubble telescope captured this and many other images.

EARTH BENEFITS FROM SPACE

Space mission science has an effect on many of our daily activities and our health. In fact, space science has had an influence on everything from baby food to drinking water. A little bit of space science benefits people here on Earth in a big way.

BEAMING HEALTH

Light-emitting diodes, or LEDs, are used to grow plants in space as they are long-lasting and make little heat. This technology is now used to improve the health of human body cells and helps patients with joint pain and muscle stiffness. NASA has developed an **infrared** ear thermometer. It measures the energy sent out by the eardrum—in the same way space scientists measure the temperature of stars.

HOLD THE FIRE

Firefighters have benefited from space science. In the United States, firefighters use air bottles made from lightweight material NASA developed for rocket casings. NASA's radio communication technology has led to strong, durable radios for firefighters. Flexible materials that resist heat, first developed by NASA, are now used in firefighters' gear.

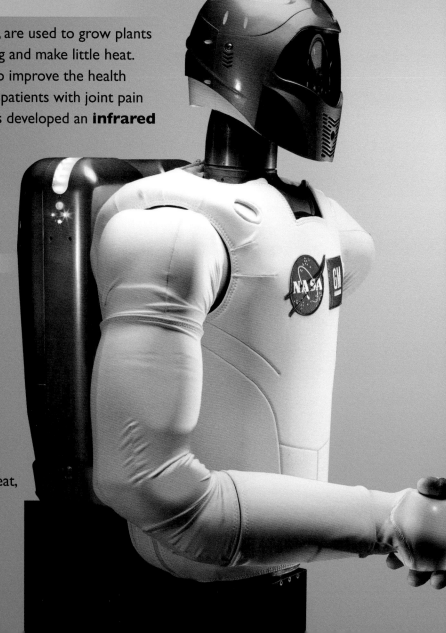

Baby food and space science? NASA research on **algae** led to the discovery of an additive full of nutrients. This is now used to enrich baby food. Technology used on the Apollo and Gemini space missions led to the development of the cordless mini-vacuum, called the Dustbuster. Space food is often freeze-dried. This reduces the weight of the food and keeps most of the nutritional value. Many backpackers now eat freeze-dried food on long hiking trips.

Robonaut 2, on the left, is in training to become an astronaut's assistant in space. One day, we may use Robonaut's skills on Earth.

Safe, drinkable water is critical to survival. NASA scientists have developed special water purification systems for the ISS. These systems have been put to use to provide clean water for poorer communities around the world.

Robonaut is a robot used on the ISS. Astronauts can use verbal commands to give Robonaut jobs to do. Robonaut's powerful computer **microchips** receive the directions, then figure out how to do the job. Robonaut can also be run by remote control. A car company wants to use Robonaut's ability to use its hands like a human to help build cars and create car-making plants that are safer.

FUTURE FANTASTIC

When the astronomer Galileo first turned his spyglass toward space in 1610, he never imagined that future scientists would invent large space telescopes that would peer into deep space. He never would have guessed that humans would walk on the Moon or think of landing on Mars. The future is here and now. Our horizons just keep expanding.

SPACE TOURISM

In the past 50 years, fewer than 600 people have traveled into space. That number is about to change. Richard Branson is a businessman. One of his companies is called Virgin Galactic. The company is working on flights to space. It will cost roughly $250,000 for a ticket. Space tourism may soon be a reality. Seven hundred people, ranging in age from 10 to over 90 years old, have already placed deposits on Virgin Galactic future flights.

The ability to hook up to an asteroid with a space exploration vehicle is close to becoming a reality.

CHANGING THE POSSIBLE

Can you imagine if astronauts could fall into a deep sleep called **torpor** and wake up just in time to land on Mars? A company named Spaceworks is proposing the design of a torpor-inducing Mars transfer habitat. It is only one of the many futuristic ideas being explored by the NASA Innovative Advanced Concepts Program.

How about satellites that build themselves in space? That is the idea behind SpiderFab. Imagine being able to remotely control the environment surrounding a rover on Mars, the Moon, or Mercury. TransFormers is a brilliant solution in which devices change their shape to unfold large, solar-reflecting panels that can light up dark craters or caves. They can reflect light to power a rover's solar panels, increasing the time spent exploring dark regions. In space, the tech possibilities are endless!

TECH TIMELINE

1957
Sputnik 1, the first spacecraft, is launched. Scientists at Canada's Defence Research Telecommunications Establishment are the first to record its beeps from space

1543
Astronomer Nicolaus Copernicus publishes his theory of the universe

1668
First reflecting telescope is built by scientist Isaac Newton

1958
NASA is formed. Explorer 1, the first American satellite to orbit Earth, is launched

1961
Yuri Gagarin of the Soviet Union becomes the first human in space

1969
Astronaut Neil Armstrong is the first human to walk on the Moon

813
School of astronomy founded in Baghdad, capital of modern-day Iraq

1666
Martian polar ice caps are noted by the astronomer Gian Domenico Cassini

1937
First radio telescope is built in the United States

1957–58
Canada and the United States build the Churchill Research Range in northern Manitoba for launching research rockets to probe the upper atmosphere

1959
Black Brant 1, the first all-Canadian research rocket, is launched

1962
Astronaut John Glenn becomes the first American to orbit Earth

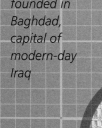

1998
John Glenn takes flight again at the age of 78— the oldest person ever to go into space

2011
Final flight of Atlantis becomes the final mission of the space shuttle program

2023
NASA Psyche spacecraft will launch on its seven-year journey to a large asteroid between Mars and Jupiter

1990
Hubble Space Telescope is launched into orbit

2013
Astronaut Chris Hadfield becomes the first Canadian Commander of the ISS

1981
Columbia, the first space shuttle, is launched into space

1971
First manned lunar rover, known as the "moon buggy"

1989
Canadian Space Agency is created

1992
The Russian government allows NASA astronauts to work on its Mir space station

2004
Cassini spacecraft arrives at Saturn

2012
NASA's Mars Science Laboratory and the Curiosity rover touch down on Mars

2018
NASA's InSight mission will launch and land on Mars to drill beneath its surface

GLOSSARY

Please note: Some **bold-faced** words are defined where they appear in the book.

algae Simple plants that grow in water

antenna A device that receives radio waves

asteroid A rocky object that travels around the Sun

astronomer A person who studies the stars, planets, and space

atmospheric pressure The pressure applied by a planet's atmosphere

cosmonauts Astronauts from Russia, formerly the Soviet Union

craters Large holes in a planet's surface

deep space The vast region of space that extends beyond the Moon, to Mars and across the solar system

elements Basic substances each made up of atoms of only one kind

geologist A person who studies the history of Earth, especially through its rocks

gravity The force that pulls things toward all planets and moons

greenhouse gases Gases in the atmosphere that contribute to the greenhouse effect that warms our planet

infrared Invisible light beyond the red end of the color spectrum

lunar Of or having to do with the Moon

microchips Groups of electronic circuits on a tiny piece of material

micrometeoroids Tiny pieces of debris flying through space

navigation The process of finding out where you are and where you need to go

orbit The path of an object around a moon or planet

osteoporosis A disease that weakens bones, especially in old age

payload The part of a spacecraft's load that includes passengers and cargo

poles The ends of the imaginary line around which Earth or another planet turns

pressurized Where the air pressure inside something is the same as it is outside

propellant A chemical or fuel that, when burned, makes something move

radiation A form of energy that can sometimes be seen as light or felt as heat

resistive Pushing or pulling against something

sensors Devices that detect or sense heat, light, sound, or motion, then react to it

solar system A sun and its planets

Soviet Union A country that existed in eastern Europe and northern Asia until 1991 —the biggest part is now what we call Russia

systems Groups of related parts that move or work together

three-dimensional (3-D) Having the three dimensions of length, width, and height

thrust The forward force produced by the engine of a rocket

torpor A state of physical or mental inactivity

LEARNING MORE

BOOKS

Dorling Kindersley/Smithsonian. *Space!* Dorling Kindersley, 2015.

Gibson, Karen Bush. *Women in Space: 23 Stories of First Flights, Scientific Missions, and Gravity-Breaking Adventures.* Chicago Review Press, 2014.

Goldsmith, Mike. *Space (Legendary Journeys).* Silver Dolphin Books, 2017.

Langley, Andrew. *Chris Hadfield and the International Space Station (Adventures in Space).* Heinemann, 2015.

WEBSITES

https://spotthestation.nasa.gov/sightings
Locate the ISS with this list of upcoming space station sighting opportunities for wherever you are.

www.asc-csa.gc.ca/eng
The website for the Canadian Space Agency is full of information, activities, and games to help you understand space and space exploration.

www.jpl.nasa.gov/education/curiosity_resources.cfm
Educational resources for students and teachers about NASA's Mars rover Curiosity, including videos, activities, and games.

www.spacefoundation.org/programs/space-technology-hall-fame
The Space Technology Hall of Fame increases public awareness of the benefits of space exploration and encourages further innovation.

About the Author

Megan Kopp is the author of more than 75 books for young readers. She would love to interview the first astronauts who make the trip to Mars.